They'

The C

MW01205213

~~~~~~ *Century*

STEPHEN R. HARPER

Urban Loft Publishers :: Portland, Oregon

They're Just Not That Into You
The Church's Struggle for Relevancy in the 21st Century

Urban Loft Publishers
2034 NE 40th Avenue #414
Portland, OR 97212
www.theurbanloft.org

Published through: CreateSpace (Amazon)
ISBN: 978-1478179146

Made in the U.S.A.

To Tara, thank you for your love and encouragement!

Contents

Foreword

Stephen Harper has a heart to reach the world for Christ. And it's that heart that compels him to speak to a church that has become so isolated and insulated from the dominant culture that it no longer speaks the same language. Indeed, it cannot because it has built too many protective barriers to truly and deeply engage.

The language of that engagement is language with which we are all familiar: it is Incarnation. Stephen makes a lot of this word, and for good reason. In the Incarnation Jesus became one of us. And not just one of us in a generic sense of becoming human: he joined a Jewish tribe in dusty Palestine at the margins of the then Roman Empire; an oppressed and downtrodden people who were mostly farmers and shepherds. Stephen makes the credible and necessary argument that there is no effective mission apart from this kind of engagement in the "thisness" and "thereness" of the world.

Having a heart to reach the world for Christ in these days when the church is so much like the world, yet so fearful of real contact, is a tough place to live. While Stephen doesn't use the phrase, much of his argument resonates with my own experience: unlearning. We must learn to be in the church, but not of it. I know – I am now using the word "church" in a less than theological sense. But that's the paradox – that the church is both a social institution, and a mystical, spiritual body. Karl Barth was fond of reminding us that "In the life of the

Christian community it can never be taken for granted that the community serves the Word of God by all its projects and institutions. The fact may be, instead, that the Word of God is being made to serve the community and its projects and institutions."[1]

This disconnect is really a big part of the problem, and the grace that comes to us in this place is a grace that arrives in the clash of cultures. The passing of the Modern world and the rise of the post-Modern, like the shift from Christendom to post-Christendom, is the grace of displacement, of liminality. We have been largely unaware of the waters in which we swim: are the fish ever aware? And so transition and displacement are a grace to God's people: we are suddenly aware of our environment, and asking new questions.

Douglas John Hall argues that we must make two parallel affirmations as we confess Christ in our post-Christendom context.[2] First, we must affirm that Jesus is Lord. Stephen reminds us (via Alan Hirsch in *The Forgotten Ways*), that this is the starting point – the solid Rock – the heart of all missional-incarnational engagement.

Second, we must affirm that God is triune. Acknowledging the triune nature of God allows us to acknowledge both the transcendence and immanence of God,

---

[1] Barth, *Evangelical Theology: An Introduction*, 191.

[2] Douglas John Hall, "Confessing Christ in a Post-Christendom Context." Address to the 1999 Covenant Conference of the Presbyterian Network, Atlanta, Georgia. November 6, 1999.

and thus allows God to maintain His radical freedom.[3] Because you see, the church, like the mission, belongs to God and not to us.

Failure to maintain this tension, like the failure to properly understand the relationship of church and kingdom, tends to place God and his mission in our control. At best we find ourselves with evangelism and mission programs out of a mechanistic and non-relational paradigm.[4] At worst we find ourselves with a God who is at our call, and who can no longer stand in judgment over every human institution, including the church. We conflate church and kingdom and create small human kingdoms that are nearly always oppressive.[5] No longer can we affirm that "the wind blows

---

[3] Paulo Suess puts it like this: "The tension between God's transcendence, on the one hand, and God's presence in the world, on the other, draws our attention to the question of the mediating divine presence. *Missio Dei* is the theological concept that allows us to speak of both the presence and transcendence of God." "Missio Dei and the Project of Jesus." *International Review of Mission*, Vol. XCII, n. 367, October 2003.

[4] As Seng-Kong Tan, "Our theological anthropology of the human person as the imago Dei cannot be seen apart from our missional theology that is centred on the *missio Dei*, as both doctrines are foundationally Trinitarian. This prevents us from constituting missions in binary terms, either as a purely humanistic enterprise or as mere divine prerogative. Rather, the church missionizes because she is missionary in nature." "A Trinitarian Ontology of Missions." *International Review of Mission*. Geneva: Apr 2004. Vol. 93, Iss. 369, 288.

[5] In *The Prophetic Imagination* Walter Brueggemann remarks that what we see in our western culture is a religion of immanence, anchored by the economics of affluence and the politics of oppression. He finds these features in Scripture in the transition of Israel from a theocracy to a monarchy, and in particular in the transition from David's rule to Solomon's, where God and the temple become a part of the royal landscape, in which the sovereignty of God is fully subordinated to the purpose of the king. From this point forward God is "on call" and access to him is controlled by the royal court. Op Cit. 31.

where it will." Rather, we know exactly what God is up to and what He approves: and it is us. On the contrary, Newbigin affirms, "The reign of God that the church proclaims is present in the life of the church, but it is not the church's possession. It goes before us, summoning us to follow."[6]

Follow we must, because we are sent as Jesus was sent (John 20:21). Through the lens of the great Celtic missionary movement, Stephen argues that a return to an older way of missional engagement is required. Like Stuart Murray, he argues that the rules of the game have changed. Where in Modernity we could invite people to believe, and then to belong, the order has changed: now we must invite them to belong, and then to believe.

People are hungry to belong; reluctant to trust that one way is right in a pluralistic context; reluctant to trust authority when so much these days is "spin." When we invite people to belong only AFTER they believe, we tend to work to ensure they have a certain list of propositions in their heads. We don't have any way to measure their hearts. It becomes too easy to push for a change in morals and intellectual assent rather than conversion of the heart. But as Hauerwas and others have reminded us, "The church does not HAVE a social strategy because the church IS a social strategy."

But it's obvious that we formed our discipleship strategies around information more than formation, around the heard

---

[6] Newbigin, *Open Secret*, 64. Likewise Glasser, *Announcing the* Kingdom, 225.

more than the heart, because we have churches full of people who can tell you what they believe, but they either do not or cannot actually live out the Gospel. We have many who would follow Jesus and who are still babies in Christ among us.

On the other hand in my church set in the urban core of Kelowna, we invited people to belong and then believe. We saw that life is caught more than taught. Not only did this approach lower the barriers to their experience of God through a people on a journey with God, it allowed them to begin to test the truth in practice. They SAW the way we loved one another. They eventually became convicted of the reality AND of the goodness of God. The social and political reality of God's reign convinced them of the truth of the Gospel. Here was a gospel that was transformative and incarnate, visible.

Stephen rightly notes that our new reality in Canada is post-Christendom. Stuart Murray points out that the distinctions in these types of social frames – belong, believe – must be understood in light of changing culture and in light of the Gospel.[7] Because "belonging" in particular is a process and because conversion, while it may have identifiable transition markers, is also a process, it's important to understand the limitations and utility of particular ecclesiological frames. We want to include all who we may, and we also want to encourage deeper commitment and

---

[7] Stuart Murray, *Church After Christendom*. (Bletchley: Paternoster Press, 2005).

faithful practice as we grow together in grace. How do we do both these things well?

It was Paul Hiebert who talked about community using set theory: bounded sets and centered sets. He saw that our current frames for understanding "membership" were inadequate. But it turns out that NEITHER the bounded set, nor the centered-set conception of community and covenant are really adequate in themselves for sustainable missional life.

In his book Stuart notes that conversion is about believing and belonging: it is both a story we commit to and a community we belong to. But as we move along in the process it is also a way of life. Moreover, belonging, believing and behaving are not different stages but different dimensions of a single journey. Progress in one dimension impacts the others, but rarely in a linear fashion.

Around the same time that *Church After Christendom* appeared, *The Shaping of Things to Come* also appeared. Starting on page 47, Frost and Hirsch open a discussion of wells and fences, using Paul Hiebert's typology of "bounded" versus "centered" sets. The authors make an explicit connection to a dynamic they describe as "attractional" and the bounded set approach to conversion. The dynamic they describe as "missional/incarnational" they relate to the centered-set mode.

In the bounded set, it is clear who is in and who is out based on a well-defined boundary – usually moral and cultural codes as well as creedal definitions – but it doesn't have much of a core definition beyond these boundaries. The bounded set is hard at the edges, soft at the center. It's like the traditional ranch with high fences. Fences keep my cattle in and keep everyone else's cattle out. Fences are mostly about possession.

The centered set, on the other hand, is like the Outback ranch with the wellspring at its center. The Outback ranch has no fences, just a water hole. There is no need to control the animals; they always come back for water. The centered set has very strong definition at the center but no boundaries. It is hard at the center, soft at the edges. In the centered set lies a clue to the structuring of new missional communities in postmodern culture.

The traditional church makes it quite difficult for people to negotiate its maze of cultural, theological, and social barriers in order to get "In," and by the time newcomers have scaled the fences built around the church, they are so socialized as churchgoers that they are not likely to be able to maintain their connection with the social groupings they came from. So we lose contact with non-believers and we lose the ability to relate to them. We extract people from their natural habitats and substitute "attractional" and "come-to" structures for missional life. (See Stephen's footnotes 5 and 6 on "come and tell" vs "go and be.")

Opposed to this extraction method, we see in the Gospels a process of Jesus challenging those who are around him, those who are listening in the various places he wanders, to deeper commitment. The group following Jesus were really a "centered set," a diverse group at various stages of belief, as well as a core group who were deeply committed to Him and His mission. We see Jesus challenging the group, to hear Him and believe Him, but also to follow Him — to take up their cross, to live in a new way, to imitate His life and proclaim the good news. So it seems that Jesus is trying to work with both a centered set and a bounded set. He wants to create a covenant community – a bounded set – within the centered set.

Stuart Murray notes that we need more than one category of belonging (37), and it is here that "membership" language – and associated practices – have failed us. Murray notes John Drane's proposal:

> [a] stakeholder model, in which there could and would be a place for diverse groups of people, who might be at different stages in their journey of faith, but who would be bound together by their commitment to one another and to the reality of the spiritual search, rather than by inherited definitions of institutional membership. (*The McDonaldization of the Church*, 159)

Murray goes on to say that centered-set churches need custodians of the story, and guardians of the ethos. Inclusivity and open-ended belonging without core maintenance is unsustainable. This is why many emerging and missional groups are considering monastic patterns based on a rule of life. They are creating a bounded set within a centered set. Groups like TOM exist around a rule, as does the Northumbria Community or The Simpler Way. We really need two structures of belonging: an open community membership and a "core" membership, open to those who voluntarily accept its demands (Murray, 37).

Interesting, this is the same argument that Roxburgh, Dietterich et al proposed in *Missional Church* in 1998.[8] It is also the same conclusion that Jim Belcher arrives at in *Deep Church*.[9]

About half way through the text, Stephen gets at the core of what it is to live as a follower of Jesus, shaped by and sharing His mission, but not isolated from the surrounding culture. He quotes from an ancient text: the Letter to Diognetus.

> For Christians are not distinguished from the rest of humanity by country, language, or custom. For nowhere do they live in cities of their own, nor do they speak some unusual dialect … But while they live in both Greek and barbarian cities … and follow the local customs in dress and food and other aspects of life, at the same time they demonstrate the remarkable and admittedly unusual character of their own citizenship. They live in their own countries, but only as aliens; they participate in everything as citizens, and endure everything as foreigners. Every foreign country is their fatherland and every fatherland is foreign. They marry like everyone else, and have children, but they do not destroy their offspring. They share their food but not their wives. They live on earth, but their citizenship is in heaven.

I'm reminded of a story Brian McLaren relates when speaking to a large group of leaders where Peter Senge

[8] Guder, *Missional Church*, 201ff.

[9] Belcher, *Deep Church,* 98ff.

appeared by video conference. Brian is interviewing Peter when he is asked, "Why do you think Buddhism is appealing to so many, and the books are selling like hotcakes, while the Christian books sit on the shelves?" Brian has no idea what to say, so he returns the question to Senge. Senge answers, "Because Christianity is presented as a set of beliefs; Buddhism is presented as a way of life."

How do we recover that way of life? And just how much trouble are we in? How isolated and insulated from the dominant culture are we? If we are going to make an attempt to re-engage, it's good to first locate ourselves, to have some way to assess just how serious the problem is.

At the close of this text, Stephen offers two inventories to help us. The second inventory is likely to see the most use, and Stephen calls it *The Church Relevancy Index*. There are five key variables:

    Friendliness
    Time use
    Language
    Visuals
    Music
    Level of Christian Enculturation
    Level of Community Connection
    Web presence

Why use this kind of tool? Because churches are often unaware of their behaviors, particularly those that may be keeping them from appealing to the community around them. They are used to what they do and how they do it and like any family, become accustomed to the idiosyncrasies and quirks that are part of their community expression. *The Church Relevancy Index* provides congregations with an outsider's view of their community and the weaknesses that those on the inside community might not notice.

I recommend Stephen's book, and his inventories, to those churches that are seeking a missional self-awareness. That should include most churches.

Dr. Len Hjalmarson
Adjunct Professor of Ministry
at Northern Baptist Theological Seminary, Chicago
and co-author of *Missional Spirituality* (IVP: 2011) and *The Missional Church Fieldbook* (Lulu.com).

What Others Are Saying

"Through rich theological reflection, sociological evaluation, scientific survey and sharing the stories of rooted Christian communities, Stephen Harper offers the Canadian - and global - church a valuable resource for engaging and adapting our faith practices for the advance of the *missio dei* in our post-modern, pluralistic realities. We need churches who are willing to release their agenda's in submission to the work Jesus desires to do in the lives of the individuals and communities we have been called. Harper's work and experience offers a framework through which to do just that."

- Jon Huckins is on staff with NieuCommunities, is the Co-Founder of The Global Immersion Project & author of *Thin Places & Teaching Through the Art of Storytelling*"

Preface

Almost everyone who has experienced the break up of a relationship or watched a romantic comedy is familiar with the line, "It's not you, it's me." What this person is really saying is that, "I'm not really that interested in you and I want to let you down easy." It's a common break up line, but when verbal communication fails, non-verbal cues take their place. When non-verbals are employed, the person in question will simply stop calling you or taking your calls. As strange as it seems, this is the situation that the church finds itself in today. As the cultures of Western Europe, the United States, Canada, Australia and New Zealand have shifted to become secular, there has been a clear message sent to the church. Except this time, the message that they are telling us is the reverse of the classic breakup line. They are saying, "It's not us, it's you."

The days of the church sharing a high degree of resonance with the surrounding culture are over. The world that we live in now is one that boasts myriad cultural expressions all contained within a complex secular matrix. This has left the church scratching its proverbial head, wondering why people don't attend anymore. The reason that people aren't going to church anymore is that *they're just not that into you*. To some, this can seem quite confusing because we live in a very "spiritual" age. Currently, there is a high interest in God, as evidenced in the Canadian context by a recent poll stating that

87 percent of Canadians still believe in God,[10] however they are less and less interested in being part of the church with each passing year. Can anything be done about this? The good news is, yes! The solution is two fold. If the church is going to once again have a voice in Canada, North America and the rest of the western world, the first thing that it must do is realize how much the world around it has changed in the last few decades, and adjust its methodologies to match. Secondly, the church must pull itself away from the comfort and trappings of its subcultural expression and re-engage the culture around it. It's only after it address these key issues that it will be able to re-engage western culture with the gospel in a significant and meaningful way.

---

[10] Bricker, *What Canadians Think*, 80.

Acknowledgements

No creative act is ever done in isolation. I would like to thank my friends and family for their support and encouragement. My professors and peers for challenging and stretching my theological pre-suppositions. Sean Benesh for his cover design. My beautiful wife and muse Tara for inspiring me to creativity far beyond what I am capable of without her. Finally, I would like to thank my Lord for adopting me into his family.

Chapter 1

The Times They Are A-Changin'

Ever since Jesus gave the command to, "go and make disciples," cultural engagement or evangelism, as it has been referred to over the years, has been one of the foundational tasks of the church. We in the evangelical wing take the task particularly seriously. We devote much time to it, spend vast sums of money both developing programs and then training people to implement those programs, not to mention the countless books written on the subject. Yet in spite of all of these efforts, we have seen fewer and fewer returns on our investment of time, talent and treasure over recent years. In fact, we have not only seen a decrease in the effectiveness of our cultural engagement methodologies in the last forty years, but we have also experienced a dramatic decrease in both church attendance and the overall amount of influence that the church has on society. The sad truth is that within the context of the western world, most people are just not that interested in the church. To put it into more colloquial terms, "they're just not that into us." So what happened?

What has happened, as Bob Dylan noted in one of his songs, is that *the times they are a-changin'.*[1] These observant words that Dylan penned in 1964 are as true now as they were then. In fact, Dylan's words carry with them both a prophetic

---

[1] Dylan, *The Times They Are A-Changin'*.

and a profound value today. The problem, simply put, is that the world has changed. "The 'modern' world which has prevailed since the enlightenment – with its cardinal principle of radical doubt, its broad rejection of the supernatural, its elevation of rationalism, its empiricism and its conviction that human nature is basically good – is on the way out."[2] We have shifted, and are still in the process of shifting, from the "modern" era to what has become known as the "postmodern era." Postmodern thought, which was first postulated by philosophers like Friedrich Nietzsche, has been around since the nineteenth century, but most sociologists agree that postmodernity started to pick up steam in the early 1960s after the assassinations of Martin Luther King Jr. and John and Robert Kennedy.[3] After these watershed events, the social climate of North America seemed to become increasingly cynical.

The church has not been without its share of events that have contributed to this growing sense of cultural cynicism. The failings of religious leaders like Jim Jones, Jimmy Swaggart, Jim Bakker and Ted Haggard, just to name a few, have all contributed toward a negative public perception of the church. As a result of these and other betrayals of trust, there has been a growing feeling of suspicion and cynicism that has become a part of the social fabric of the United States and

---

[2] Green, *Evangelism in the Early Church*, 11.

[3] Halter and Smay, *The Tangible Kingdom*, 63.

Canada. In fact, in a recent Canadian poll almost ninety percent of Canadians say they trust their doctors, but only sixty-five percent said that they trust church representatives.[4] This distrust of its leaders has far-reaching ramifications for the church.

One of the primary implications of this climate of distrust is that we must now begin the process of cultivating relationships and earning confidence before people listen to us. For this reason, cultural engagement must transition from its historic presentation and attractional mode[5] to an almost completely relational and missional approach.[6] After all, if we do not have their trust, they will not hear us and if they do not hear us, how will they believe? It is because of this shift that the methodologies and practices which worked in the past will continue to become less and less effective as we move further into this new era.

Unfortunately, in the midst of these massive seismic cultural shifts, church leaders and individual Christians in most denominations have either been oblivious, indifferent or in complete denial to the obvious changes occurring around

---

[4] Leger Marketing, "How Canadians Perceive Various Professions," 11.

[5] Sweet, *So Beautiful*, 18. The attractional church can be summed up by the words, *come and tell*. It "assumes that if they build it, and build it hip and cool, people will come," and once people come to the church the attractional mode relies on a propositional and presentational method of communicating the Gospel.

[6] The Missional approach can be summed up by the words, *go and be*. It is a proactive approach that is focused on going out to engage culture rather than waiting for culture to come to the church building.

them. In fact, it seems that in Canada the evangelical church has gone so far as to have retreated into itself and become a sub-culture instead of the countercultural movement it is meant to be. For example, it seems to be more and more common for Canadian Christians to have only Christian friends, read Christian books, listen almost exclusively to Christian music and send their kids to Christian schools.[7] Not that there is anything wrong with these things in and of themselves. However, in many cases they have become a fortress, which enables Christians to hide from the culture around them, rather than engage it. Further, it is in this context that many times cultural engagement creates conformity to the church sub-culture rather than a call to a counter-cultural life.

Cultural engagement, or evangelism in the modern world has been expressed in a variety of ways that for the most part can be put into one of two camps – mass evangelism or seeker evangelism.[8] The dominant method of evangelism over the last 150 years has been the evangelistic crusade. And though it has gone by other names, like tent meetings or revivals, and has had minor content updates over the years, the overall idea has remained the same. The premise is to hold a big event with a dynamic speaker and invite all of the "non-Christians" to come and get "saved." For example, when we think of evangelistic methods, we might picture men like Billy Graham

---

[7] A personal observation from 20 years of ministry in a variety of settings.

[8] Webber, *The Younger Evangelicals*, 216.

preaching in a church building or perhaps a great arena.[9] In fact, in the context of mass attractional evangelism, "Charles G. Finney and Billy Graham are bookends. What Charles G. Finney, the father of modern urban mass evangelism started, Billy Graham ended."[10]

In the last couple of decades, the crusade event has been replaced by an ongoing Sunday service format change called the "seeker sensitive" approach, which has usually meant toning down the content of the worship service in order to make "seekers" who may be in attendance more comfortable. Both of these approaches have been effective in the past and many have come to faith in the highly emotive environment of a crusade or the "user-friendly" environment of the seeker approach of the 80s and 90s. However, the world has changed. We can no longer expect the outside world to come to us, as we have in the past.

Virtually all the historic Protestant denominations in Britain, Australia, New Zealand, Canada and the United States are in serious decline. In fact, it has been reported that "church attendance in Britain has declined from 7.5 percent in 1998 to 6.3 percent in 2007, and it is projected to continue declining."[11] On the other side of the Atlantic, *The Pew Forum on Religion and Public Life* places weekly attendance in

---

[9] Green, *Evangelism*, 300.

[10] Sweet, *Soul Tsunami*, 95.

[11] Sine, *The New Conspirators*, 205.

Canada at 18 percent and at 35 percent in the United States.[12] Pollsters like Darrell Bricker back up this fact. In his book *What Canadians Think*, he claims that since 1949 weekly church attendance has dropped in half from 40 percent to a meager 20 percent.[13] Bricker goes further, saying that while Canadians' belief in God is still quite high at 87 percent, a full 81 percent of Canadians "agree that you don't have to go to church to be a good Christian."[14] This would indicate that for Canadians the problem is not so much with God but with the church. The fact is – the church has an image problem.

---

[12] Ibid.

[13] *What Canadians Think*, 80.

[14] Ibid.

PART I

A Change In Our Methods

Chapter 2

The Blueprint for Cultural Engagement

As we move further into the uncharted waters of the postmodern world, it is becoming increasingly clear to many Christian leaders and thinkers that the methods used in the past to engage the culture outside the walls of the church are no longer effective. I believe that if we are to break free of the current malaise, we must re-examine biblical principles in order to find an effective way to once again proclaim God's never-changing word to an ever changing world. With that in mind, the understanding of three main theological concepts will serve as the blueprint for this approach. It is my belief that for cultural engagement to be effective in a postmodern context it must be: Incarnational,[1] Relational/Missional,[2] and Adaptive.

---

[1] Hirsch, *The Forgotten Ways*, 281. This book will use Allan Hirsch's definition of *incarnational* as it appears on page 281 of his book. This definition has a two-fold meaning. First, the Incarnation, "refers to the act of God in entering into the created universe and realm of human affairs as the man Jesus of Nazareth." Second, being *incarnational* means "embodying the culture and life of a target group in order to meaningfully reach that group of people from within their culture."

[2] Ibid., 285. The definition of *missional* that this book will use will likewise draw from Allan Hirsch's definition on page 285 of his book, *The Forgotten Ways*. Hirsch defines being *missional*, in relation to the church, as being "a church that defines itself, and organizes its life around, its real purpose as an agent of God's mission to the world." In this context being missional takes its cue from the incarnation and is always going out to engage culture.

The first of these theological rationales is the appreciation that the event of the incarnation sets the example of how God desires both individual Christians and His church to relate to the world. God came to us – he expects us to do the same with others. Next, as followers of Jesus we have been given the mission to make the "Good News" known to all people but we are to carry out this task in an attitude and posture of love. The third and last theological concept, which undergirds this approach, is the belief that God has given us as human beings, individual Christians and the church the ability to adapt and change how we share the gospel in light of the different cultures or cultural dynamics that we may encounter. It is only after we integrate these concepts into our understanding of cultural engagement that we will be able to rise up to effectively meet the challenges of engaging the postmodern culture. Finally, let us be clear about the fact that, "postmodernism is the context we work in, not the goal."[3]

The Incarnation Sets the Evangelistic Example We Should Follow

When thinking about how the church goes about engaging any culture with the gospel, we cannot escape the fact that "God is a missionary – He sent His son into our world, into our lives, into human history."[4] The "incarnation therefore

---

[3] Webber, *Younger Evangelicals*, 219.

[4] Frost and Hirsch, *The Shaping of Things to Come*, 39.

implies some form of sending, in order to be able to radically incarnate into the various contexts in which disciples live."[5] The incarnation is therefore arguably the most important theological concept in the whole Bible. It is here that God not only communicates how He is going to reconcile humanity and all of creation with Himself, but also provides us with the example of how we are to continue Jesus' work after His ascension.

The Gospel of John begins with important theological statements in that regard. In fact, it is for this reason that "John 1:14 is one of the most significant verses in the Bible."[6] It is in John's Gospel that we are told about the *logos or eternal Word*, who was ever-existent with God, and through whom all things were created. The fact that John has written it this way is of critical importance. For "if the evangelist had said only that the eternal Word assumed manhood or adopted the form of a body, the reader steeped in the popular dualism of the time might have missed the point."[7] "But John is unambiguous, almost shocking in the expressions he uses: the *Word became flesh*."[8]

However, the evangelist did not stop there with his direct description of the Christ event. He goes on to tie the *logos* (the

---

[5] Ibid.

[6] Burge, *John, NIV Application Commentary,* 59.

[7] Carson, *The Gospel According to John*, 126.

[8] Ibid.

divine Word of God) becoming flesh with the Greek word *skene*, which means, "tabernacle." This word carries with it weighty historical and theological inferences, and is used in the *Septuagint* (the Greek version of the Hebrew Bible) to describe God's presence that Israel experienced in the desert. The evangelist is implying that now "God has chosen to dwell amongst his people in a yet more personal way, in the Word-becoming-flesh."[9] "In other words, Christ is the locus of God's dwelling with Israel as He had dwelt with them in the desert."[10] The Old Testament symbolism of that event should not be lost. Once again, God has manifested His presence, but this time it is the powerful and tangible presence of His son. The *logos* came and made His dwelling among us, or as Eugene Peterson phrases it in *The Message*, "the Word became flesh and blood, and moved into the neighborhood."[11]

When considering the incarnation and how it pertains to the question of cultural engagement in a postmodern world, we must include an appreciation of both its literal and figurative meanings. Understanding the literal ramifications of the incarnation means that we must keep in mind and realize that God is at work in the world and in the lives of individuals before we arrive on the scene. Secondly, understanding the incarnation in a figurative sense means that we need to be

---

[9] Ibid., 127.

[10] *John*, 59.

[11] John 1:14 *(The Message)*.

present and engaged with those we are trying to minister to. This two-fold understanding is crucial because it brings fullness to the comprehension of the importance of the incarnation. The former shows us how God engages humanity and the latter shows us how we are supposed to do it.

The first reality of the incarnation is that in a very literal sense, God is working behind the scenes all of the time. This concept, which has been referred to in such terms as prevenient grace, is one of the keys to postmodern evangelism. It is, "recognizing that God is already at work in people's lives before we 'arrive on the scene,' and that our role is helping people to see how God is present and active in their lives, calling them home."[12] This idea of God being active before His representatives arrived on the scene was one of the hallmarks of the evangelistic practices of St. Patrick. "Celtic missionaries seem to have believed that God's prevenient grace had preceded them and prepared the people for the gospel."[13] This theological concept, which was taken for granted by the Celtic missionaries, has also been noted by numerous present day biblical scholars and theologians. One of the most notable of late is Henry Blackaby, who comments in his book *Experiencing God*, that God is at work all around us.[14] According to Blackaby, our decision as both the church

---

[12] Sweet, *Soul Tsunami*, 55.

[13] Hunter, *The Celtic Way of Evangelism*, 92.

[14] Blackaby and King, *Experiencing God*, 50.

and as individual believers is not whether to do evangelism or not, but whether to join God in what He is already doing.[15]

The second reality of the incarnation is that, in a figurative sense, we must heed Jesus' example and be actively involved with the world around us. However, as noted before, too often the church today lacks any real and tangible connection to the world around it. To be involved with those around us in an evangelistic capacity requires one thing: love. As author Leonard Sweet warns us, "Evangelism doesn't require training. Evangelism requires love. Lack of evangelism means lack of love."[16]

Jesus' Followers Have Been Given a Mission of Love
The Mission

When it comes to trying to inspire Christians to go out and do the work of cultural engagement, one of the most quoted portions of scripture is found in the Gospel of Matthew. In the twenty-eighth chapter of Matthew's Gospel, Jesus says, "All authority in heaven and on earth has been given to me. Therefore go and make disciples of all nations, baptizing them in the name of the Father and of the Son and of the Holy Spirit, and teaching them to obey everything I have commanded you. And surely I am with you always, to the very

---

[15] Ibid.

[16] *Soul Tsunami*, 60.

end of the age.[17] This important passage has been used to inspire "Christian mission" for good reason. "The five short verses that comprise the Great Commission passage are among the most important to establish the ongoing agenda of the church throughout the ages."[18]

It is clear from this portion of scripture that "the disciple's central responsibility is to reproduce themselves."[19] Cultural engagement and discipleship are important features of the gospel and have been primary tenets of the church since the earliest of times, as echoed by all of the gospel writers. In the context of Matthew's account, this is the third time that he uses the Greek verb *matheteuo*. On the first two occasions the verb had a passive tense.[20] "Here the verb takes on a distinctively transitive sense, 'make a disciple,' in which the focus is on calling individuals to absolute commitment to the person of Jesus as one's sole Master and Lord."[21]

Matthew further emphasizes the importance of making disciples by the grammatical make up of the passage. For, "the Great Commission contains one primary, central command, the imperative 'make disciples,' with three subordinate

---

[17] Matt. 28:18-20 (NIV).

[18] Wilkins, *Matthew, NIV Application Commentary,* 947.

[19] Turner, *Matthew, Baker Exegetical Commentary on the New Testament,* 689.

[20] *Matthew, NIV Application Commentary,* 952.

[21] Ibid.

participles."[22] "These subordinate participles take on imperatival force because of the imperative main verb and so characterize the ongoing mandatory process of discipleship to Jesus."[23] So because Jesus now exercises universal authority,[24] his "disciples must go out and engage in the universal mission to make disciples of all nations."[25]

The importance and mission of this scripture verse has not changed. What has changed, as we transition into this new epoch, is the emphasis and the way that we reach the destination of making disciples. For the last two hundred years this passage has been read as a list of things to do: "go," "make disciples," and "baptize." The modern emphasis has been on what disciples are to be doing. However, for the postmodern reader the emphasis shifts from what we are going to do, to how we are going to do it. This question of "how" will require us to rethink some crucial components of our approach to cultural engagement, such as our goals and how we define success. For in a postmodern context, motive is just as important as method and how/why we do something is more important that what we do.

---

[22] Ibid., 951.

[23] Ibid.

[24] Matt. 22:18 (NIV).

[25] *Matthew*, *NIV Application Commentary,* 952.

The Motive

It is because of this question of "proper motives" that I believe in a postmodern context the Great Commission is to be carried out in light of the Great Commandment. Matthew 22:36-40 states: "Love the Lord your God with all your heart and with all your soul and with all your mind.' This is the first and greatest commandment. And the second is like it: 'Love your neighbor as yourself.' All the Law and the Prophets hang on these two commandments." This is a key verse in the Bible because it is here that Jesus gives us hints about what should motivate us to go about making disciples: love. Jesus emphasizes this point by stating that just behind loving God, loving our neighbor is the greatest commandment.

"Love for one's neighbor means acting toward others with their good, their well-being, their fulfillment, as the primary motivation and goal of our deeds."[26] "In the same way that individuals are called to care for themselves responsibly and attune their lives to carry out God's will in their lives, they are to give themselves to others to care for them responsibly and help them attune their lives to carry out God's will."[27] "Jesus is not simply advocating an emotional attachment or an abstract love," but rather, "a concrete responsibility": "an act of being useful and beneficial to one's neighbor."[28] Donald

---

[26] Hagner, *Matthew 14-28*, *Word Biblical Commentary,* 648.

[27] *Matthew*, *NIV Application Commentary,* 725.

[28] Ibid.

Hagner notes, "that loving God entails reverence and obedience whereas loving humans entails serving them and seeking their well-being."[29] "What is more, the proper motivation for correct interpersonal relationships always remains a profound sense of gratitude for what God has done for us in Christ."[30] "Love is an unconditional commitment to an imperfect person in which one gives oneself to another to bring the relationship to God's intended purposes."[31]

This carries massive consequences for the Christian church because throughout history, both individual Christians and the church, have used methods of cultural engagement that have been contrary to how Jesus would have had us go about evangelism and discipleship. What loving our neighbors as ourselves doesn't mean is that, even with the best of intentions, cultural engagement should occur at the end of a sword of a conquering army, as was the practice during post-Constantinian Imperial Rome, the Crusades or the Spanish Inquisition. It should also not occur simultaneously with Colonial expansion as happened with the Western European exploration/exploitation of the new world, where colonial missionaries sought to "civilize" the "savages."

More recently, it has also been argued that cultural engagement shouldn't take place from the position of the

---

[29] *Matthew, 14-28, Word Biblical Commentary,* 648.

[30] Blomberg, *Matthew, The New American Commentary,* 333-334.

[31] *Matthew, NIV Application Commentary,* 726.

hollow "sales pitch" techniques that have been used in the last century. Granted, these are all extreme examples of some of the church's darker times. However, what unfortunately sticks in the minds of the un-churched is not when the church is at its best but when the church is at its worst. If we are going to engage postmodern culture successfully in the twenty-first century, we will need to do it with an attitude and posture of love. We must love our neighbors without strings, without agenda and in spite of any behaviors that we might not like or agree with. This level of authenticity cannot be faked.

God Gives Us the Ability to Adapt and Change Our Approach to Cultural Engagement

The third and final theological rationale is the fact that God has given us the ability to adapt and change how we share the gospel in light of the different cultures or cultural dynamics that we encounter. A scripture passage that emphasizes the importance of the contextualization process is 1 Corinthians 9:19-23. It is here that Paul gives examples of the different people groups that he has adapted to, in order to contextually present the gospel.

> Though I am free and belong to no man, I make myself a slave to everyone, to win as many as possible. To the Jews I became like a Jew, to win the Jews. To those under the law I became like one under the law (though I myself am not under the law), so as to win those under the law. To those not having the law I became like one not having the law (though I am not free from God's law but am under Christ's law), so as to win those not having the law. To the weak I became weak, to win the weak. I have become all

things to all men so that by all possible means I might save some.

After he has listed these groups, he then gives the conclusion and the purpose for his commitment to adaptability, "so that by all possible means he might save some." This verse makes plain the evangelistic principle underlying Paul's contextual attitude[32] toward the various pre-Christian people groups that he encountered on his journey. For whatever he does, "he wants to clear the ground of unnecessary obstacles that might hinder unbelievers from coming to Christ."[33]

This inventory of people groups that Paul has contextualized his gospel presentation for should have been familiar to his original readers since, "all the members of the Corinthian congregation at one time fell into one of the categories that Paul lists."[34] However, in the years after the birth of the Corinthian congregation there crept in an unhealthy level of competition, spiritual elitism and many deep divisions between the church's members. Consequently, it seems many of them had forgotten where they came from and how they used to live before they heard the gospel. It is in light of these prevailing attitudes and divisions that Paul's

---

[32] Blomberg, *1 Corinthians*, *The NIV Application Commentary*, 183.

[33] Ibid.

[34] Garland, *1 Corinthians*, *Baker Exegetical Commentary on the New Testament*, 429.

actions, which might have appeared inconsistent to the readers in the Corinthian church, "have an integrity at a much higher level."[35] He is reminding his readers of many things in this letter, among them, the fact his freedom as an Apostle, and ours for that matter, enables him to adapt and contextualize his message so that many may hear.

The principle that Paul outlines in 1 Corinthians 9:19-23 does not imply duplicity or manipulation, but merely that he "shares the condition of those to whom he ministers, and so is conformed to the pattern of his Lord."[36] Paul is careful not to change the message, only its presentation. For in his approach, "he is intransigent on matters that affect the gospel itself, whether theological or behavioral, that same concern for the saving power of the gospel is what causes him to become all things to all people in matters that don't count."[37] "So we dare not apply his strategy of all things to all people to issues of fundamental morality or immorality."[38] "But in the morally gray areas of life, such as eating food sacrificed to idols and their numerous cultural equivalents in any era, Paul bends over backwards to be sensitive to the non-Christian mores of society around him in order not to hinder people from

---

[35] Fee, *The First Epistle to the Corinthians*, *The New International Commentary on the New Testament*, 431.

[36] *1 Corinthians*, *Baker Exegetical Commentary on the New Testament*, 436.

[37] *First Corinthians*, *The New International Commentary on the New Testament*, 431.

[38] *1 Corinthians*, *The NIV Application Commentary*, 186.

accepting the gospel."[39] It is only when contextualization of the gospel is practiced that, "Christianity stands the best chances of being understood and even accepted."[40]

Craig Blomberg reminds us that one of the biggest obstacles that we face is, "overcoming non-Christian misconceptions about the nature of Christianity."[41] These misconceptions that, "more often than not involve legalism rather than license, form a crucial part of the evangelistic process and make the Christian claims of freedom and joy more credible."[42] Blomberg adds, "sadly, Christians of many eras have instead tended to be more sensitive to the legalism of fellow church members and have too quickly censured contemporary social customs, alienating themselves from the very people they should have been trying to win to Christ."[43] An example of this could be early colonial missionaries in Africa requiring the indigenous peoples to adopt a Victorian style of dress. The impetus came from the missionaries' own sense of modesty and propriety, ignoring the practicality, culture and custom of the Africans. Many times in history we have attempted to engage the culture around us and have used

---

[39] Ibid.

[40] Ibid.

[41] Ibid., 187.

[42] Ibid.

[43] Ibid., 186.

methods that are viewed by those we are trying to talk to, as insincere.

In light of these verses, "it is hard to justify the prevailing pattern of evangelism by formula: using tracts, sets of questions, or prepackaged approaches on everyone with whom we want to share Christ."[44] This verse challenges us to think contextually outside of the box. "We're going to have to learn all the things we can do instead of limiting ourselves based on a few things we're warned to avoid."[45]

These verses have "massive implications for the strategies of outreach and friendships with unbelievers, though they can be exaggerated."[46] A helpful way of understanding what Paul meant when he instructed us to become *all things to all people* is to connect this expression with one of Jesus' favorite metaphors for his gospel, "water," or "living water."[47] Water can take many different shapes without sacrificing its integrity. Likewise, the church should be able to take many different shapes in its effort to adapt to the myriad new situations that it finds itself in.

"The keys to postmodern ministry are adaptability, flexibility, and speed, which might be defined as the ability to

---

[44] Ibid., 188.

[45] Halter and Smay, *The Tangible Kingdom*, 137.

[46] *1 Corinthians*, *The NIV Application Commentary*, 185-186.

[47] Sweet, *So Beautiful*, 183.

change midstream,"[48] and unless we can learn these skills the church will continue to flounder in the postmodern mire that it is now in.

---

[48] *Soul Tsunami*, 97.

Chapter 3

The Approach to Cultural Engagement

Much has been written in the past decade about how much western society has changed as it transitioned from the modern to the postmodern world. However, during the last century the evangelical church has changed a great deal as well. It has gone from being the predominant cultural expression to one of many subcultures within the larger North American milieu. Interestingly, much of this relegation to the cultural sidelines is a product of the church's own doing.

There have been many theories on what has caused the evangelical church to pull away and diverge so dramatically from the larger culture, but it is generally agreed that one of the key events that contributed to the church changing its posture toward "the world" was the outcome of the "Scopes Monkey Trial" of 1925.[1] It is here that the initial break seems to have occurred, and as a result the church entered into a period of isolation from, and suspicion of the outside world. Recently, there has been a move to reverse this long-standing trend with the advent of the neo-evangelical "missional" movement. University of Denver Professor Carl Raschke

---

[1] The Scopes Monkey Trial was an American legal case that challenged the Tennessee law that made it illegal to teach anything but creationism in the school system. For more on the historical account and relevance of the Scopes Trial see Edward J. Larson, *Summer for the Gods: The Scopes Trial and America's Continuing Debate Over Science and Religion* (Cambridge, Massachusetts: Basic Books, 2006).

comments on this phenomenon in his book *GloboChrist* when he says:

> One of the shibboleths of the new evangelicalism is engaging the culture. This phrase frequently implies that the faithful in years gone by have walled themselves off from wider cultural practices and trends and established their own ghetto, a distinctive Christian subculture. If one examines the history of American evangelicalism in the twentieth century, that conclusion is surely justified. The Scopes Monkey Trial of 1925 was the turning point in American history that led to the formation of such ghetto. When American evangelicals, who once proudly referred to themselves as "fundamentalists," were publically humiliated by Scope's brilliant attorney Clarence Darrow in their effort to defend the literal truth of Genesis against evolutionary science, evangelicals became disheartened; history shows that they quickly beat a broad and sullen retreat into a Christian ghetto.[2]

We must attempt to break free of the "ghetto" mentality that fuels the Christian subculture for many in North America. The fact is, when it comes to engaging the culture around them, "many Christians barely know any non-Christians well enough to share their faith in less than a superficial fashion,"[3] and if these behaviors are left unchecked they will only work to further deepen the rift that now stands between the church and the larger North American culture, into a vast crevice. In his book *The Forgotten Ways*, Alan Hirsch refers to this concept as "cultural distance,"[4] and the greater the degree of

---

[2] Raschke, *GloboChrist*, 57.

[3] Blomberg, *1 Corinthians*, *The NIV Application Commentary*, 189.

[4] Hirsch, *The Forgotten Ways*, 56.

cultural distance, the harder the church will have to work to connect with the world around it. This will greatly affect how we go about engaging the culture outside of the church.

It is because of these cultural shifts, we need to change our methods and our mindset toward evangelism in three primary ways. First, we must shift from being attractional to being incarnational. Second, we must shift from living apart from the larger culture to dwelling with it. Third, we must shift from copying the methodologies of others to discovering our own contextual ways to lovingly engage the larger culture around us. Few would argue that these are indeed difficult times for the church in the western world. However, as Albert Einstein said, "in the middle of difficulty lies opportunity,"[5] and the opportunity before us is vast.

From Attractional to Incarnational

Most cultural engagement methodologies are designed with a "come and hear" mentality. If we are to be effective in the twenty-first century we must lay aside this outmoded method in favor of a different paradigm, one which embraces an incarnational approach. An incarnational approach to engaging the culture around us requires us to adopt a "go and be" instead of a "come and hear" mentality. This attitude will focus on listening to and journeying with pre-Christians within the context of an ongoing relationship.

---

[5] Frédérick Jézégou, "Quotations by Albert Einstein."

45

However, one of the obstacles that will continue to hinder us from successfully shifting from an attractional to an incarnational approach is that we have almost exclusively defined our "God experience" in terms of a building. An author once wrote that the "Church" suffers from an edifice complex,[6] and to a certain extent this is true. Examples of this can be found in almost any societal setting. Even our strategies to go out and reach the lost are defined on these attractional building-centric terms. Cultural engagement in this context, "is primarily about mobilizing church members to attract unbelievers into church where they experience God. Rather than being '*out-reach,*' it effectively becomes '*in-drag.*'"[7] What must change in our new context is the fact that, "incarnational believers must search for ways to connect not just to each other but to the world beyond the church."[8]

Yet, the reality is when we talk about cultural engagement and planting churches, our actions often betray our institutional mindset. Nearly all of our methods are designed to lure people into our buildings. Whether we admit it or not "one of the core assumptions that the attractional church is based upon, is the assumption that God cannot really be accessed outside the sanctioned church meetings or, at the very least, that these meetings are the best place for not-yet-

---

[6] Reid, *Introduction to Evangelism*, 94.

[7] *The Shaping of Things to Come*, 41.

[8] McNeal, *Missional Renaissance*, 50.

Christians to learn about God."[9] Simply put, the problem is that, "the gospel says 'Go' but our church buildings say, 'Stay'. The gospel says, 'Seek the lost,' but our churches say, 'Let the lost seek the church.'"[10] The truth is that we are addicted to buildings and if we are going to be successful in the twenty-first century we must break this cycle by redefining and expanding our idea of what "church" is. We must endeavor to engage in an ongoing ministry outside of our traditional structural walls because whether we want to admit it or not, people are not coming into our buildings anymore.

In the last fifty years, the church in the western world has experienced an ever-decreasing amount of effectiveness carrying out its mission of making "disciples of all nations." One of the primary reasons for this phenomenon is that many, if not most of the current evangelistic methodologies used by the church aren't designed to deal with postmodern cultural dynamics. "Most churches in the evangelical wing of the church sincerely long to have an impact on their world, but they are somehow stuck in the same systems story that binds them to past practices."[11] Traditional evangelical cultural engagement models such as the crusade, the revival, High Holiday services, special topical event speakers/services and even programs like small group ministries are all based on an

---

9 *The Shaping of Things to Come*, 41.

10 Ibid., 69.

11 Bergquist and Karr, *Church Turned Inside Out,* viii.

attractional model. The attractional model assumes that those outside the church are interested in and are attracted to what is happening in the church or the various programs that it may offer. This model has worked in the past because there has been a high resonance between the culture of the church and that of the larger society. In the past, most people had a paradigm that still included the Judeo–Christian understanding of God.

However, we no longer live in that world. We live in a world where we are seeing an ever-increasing dissonance between these views. "In the old model of evangelism, we build friendships, call people to conversion at some evangelistic event and then involve them in Christian fellowship and discipleship."[12] This must change because as stated earlier, there is a growing chasm between the church and culture, and people aren't coming to these events anymore. To do this "go and be" and "go and do" must be the emphasis for the Church not "come and hear." For, "demonstration has replaced proclamation as the way to gain a hearing for the gospel,"[13] and incarnational presence has replaced attractional invitation as a platform of proclaiming the gospel. "Incarnational mission will mean that in reaching a people group we will need to identify with them in all ways

---

[12] Richardson, *Evangelism Outside the Box*, 76.

[13] *Missional Renaissance*, 33.

possible without compromising the truth of the gospel itself."[14]

From Living Apart to Dwelling With

It is for this reason that we must start defining church as "where we are," instead of "where we go." Church in the twenty-first century must be missional and incarnational, "not attractional, in its ecclesiology."[15] After all, "God's mission has been most clearly revealed in the incarnation,"[16] and in a postmodern setting being present and involved in the lives of individuals will be better received and more effective than trying to devise ways to entice them into following us back to our buildings, because they are no longer interested in coming to our buildings.

One of the best historical examples of incarnational engagement is found in the early Celtic church. Incarnational engagement was a concept that was both embraced and employed by St. Patrick. This approach was so successful that it transformed Ireland from a pagan to a Christian nation within a couple of generations. Under Patrick, the early Celtic teams would upon arrival at a tribal settlement, "engage the king and other opinion leaders, hoping for their conversion, or at least their clearance, to camp near the people and form into

---

[14] *The Shaping of Things to Come*, 37.

[15] Ibid., 12.

[16] *Missional Renaissance*, 22.

a community of faith adjacent to the tribal settlement."[17] In the early Irish missionary effort the ministry team would spend months working as a "ministering community of faith within the tribe,"[18] and then would establish a permanent indigenous presence when the larger portion of the ministry team moved to the next village. By setting up a permanent indigenous presence, Patrick ensured that the conversation would continue.

These ideas of conversation and dialog are as important in our current situation as they were in the early Celtic church. Like the early Celts, we now live in a pluralistic society. We are faced with many competing value and belief systems, and "in a pluralistic society, the possibility of conversion is opened up through conversations with people who live with a contrasting view of reality."[19] It is for this reason that we must be willing to venture out from the safety of our comfort zone in order to engage those in the larger North American culture.

This is a concept that was put forward by renowned sociologist Peter Berger in his groundbreaking book, *The Social Construction of Reality*. He gives three main sociological insights which underline the importance of incarnational/missional evangelism. According to Berger, a person's view of reality is largely shaped and maintained by

---

[17] Hunter, *The Celtic Way of Evangelism*, 21.

[18] Ibid., 22.

[19] Ibid., 99.

the community into which one has been socialized. Yet in a pluralistic society, one can begin to experience changes to his or her reality through conversations with people who live with a contrasting view. And one adopts and internalizes the new worldview through re-socialization into a community sharing that new worldview. [20]

This is key because if we are going to be as effective in reaching out to those outside of the church, we must first start by realizing that each of us looks at the world in a unique way. Indeed, "at the base of all our thought – all our ruminations about God, ourselves and the world around us is a world view." [21] When people come to Christ they are not simply changing their mind on something. They are altering a portion of, if not all of their worldview. These facts about our social construction of reality make incarnational/missional evangelism all the more important. In other words, if the unchurched are willing to simply hang out with Christians, they will in turn come in contact with God, and if they come in contact with God they will be changed by the experience. That's not to say that this is a completely passive approach, but is meant to emphasize the fact that there is a vicarious effect that comes from coming in contact with God's Spirit through God's people.

---

[20] Berger and Luckmann, *The Social Construction of Reality*, 166-169.

[21] Sire, *Naming the Elephant*, 18.

The early Celtic missionaries were familiar with this concept. They "believed that God's prevenient grace had preceded them and prepared the people for the gospel."[22] They realized that "most people experience the faith through relationships, that they encounter the gospel through a community of faith."[23] For the ancient Irish people and for today's "postmoderns, participation and conversation come before conversion."[24] This stands in stark contrast to the way that things were being done in Patrick's time by the Catholic Church. "Roman Christians preached, called for a decision, and then began churches when people believed. Celtic Christians, by contrast, invited people into their monastic communities to belong before they believed."[25] "Participants in the inviting community will seek to draw others to Christ by embodying that gospel in the fellowship they share."[26] After all, as St. Augustine said "faith is caught not taught" and "for most people, belonging comes before believing."[27]

We must live and walk with the people that we are ministering to with an incarnational presence. "You cannot

---

[22] *The Celtic Way of Evangelism*, 92.

[23] Ibid., 54.

[24] Sweet, *Soul Tsunami*, 55.

[25] *Evangelism Outside the Box*, 59.

[26] Grenz, *A Primer on Postmodernism*, 169.

[27] *The Celtic Way of Evangelism,* 54.

become part of the organic life of a given community if you are not present to it and do not experience its cultural rhythms, its life and its geography."[28] Part of the reason that St. Patrick was so successful in reaching the Irish with the gospel is because he gave himself to Ireland. He became one of them and moved to the rhythm of their culture and so was able to communicate with them in a manner that they could understand. One of the problems that we have today is that those in the church live near to pre-Christians but not with pre-Christians. We have cut ourselves off from the world and made a little Christian ghetto to live in, free of much contact with the outside world. In light of this, it is understandable to see how cultural engagement has been reduced to a confrontation between two foes. We must remember that it's not us and them, it's just us.

From Impersonation to Innovation

In order to stay relevant to the unchurched culture around us we must continually adapt how we present our never changing message to an ever-changing world. After all, no two audiences, no two churches, no two people, no two situations are the same. "One of greatest challenges of the future is for the church to move from franchise mentality to create-your-own app."[29] The truth is, what works in Los Angeles doesn't

---

[28] *The Shaping of Things to Come*, 39.

[29] Leonard Sweet, quote from *Twitter*, October 29, 2009.

necessarily translate to Toronto, and we must stop pretending that it will. Admittedly, there are principles contained within most methodologies that can be applied in a variety of situations. But as the cultural distance grows between church and culture and North American society moves farther from its Judeo-Christian roots, the issue of context becomes even more acute. Like the real estate axiom that states the three most important rules are location, location, location -- the three most important rules when thinking about cultural engagement in the twenty-first century are context, context, context.

A good example of the need to be contextual in the face of this growing cultural distance and diversity can be found in my adopted hometown of Vancouver, British Columbia. Vancouver is arguably one of the most diverse cities in the world, and British Columbia is Canada's most ethnically diverse province.[30] The Greater Vancouver Regional District (or GVRD for short) is home to a high percentage of visible minorities, though European ("white"), minorities such as German, Dutch, Slavic and Mediterranean peoples are numerous as well. The 2006 census showed that 41.7 percent of the GVRD population was of visible minority origin, the largest group being the Chinese followed by South Asians.[31] Other prominent minority groups such as Filipino, Korean, Japanese, Southeast Asian, West Asian and Latin American are

---

[30] Statistics Canada 2006. "Population Distribution of Vancouver, B.C."

[31] Ibid.

also present in large numbers in the GVRD. Though the GVRD is a small geographic area, (only fifty miles in diameter from East to West),[32] what works in one of these areas will not necessarily work in the others.

For example, what works with the young urban professionals who live in the downtown core will not work with the neo-bohemians who live in East Van,[33] which is only a few miles away, and what works with the suburban Anglo population of Langley will likely not work with the Indo-Canadian population of Surrey or the predominantly Chinese population of Richmond. In this new world, "for anything to be real it must be local."[34]

The concept of contextualizing our cultural engagement strategies is nothing new. In fact, one of the reasons that Paul's preaching was so authoritative was because he had a knack for picking the master metaphor that mattered locally.[35] This is a concept that is also true throughout history because all of "the great preachers of the past were those who belonged so deeply to their time that they could speak to their times."[36] We must

---

[32] Geographic information provided by Metro Vancouver; available from http://www.metrovancouver.org/about/statistics/Pages/default.aspx.

[33] East Van is the nickname for the area of Vancouver that is east of Main Street and goes to Boundary Road.

[34] Sweet, *So Beautiful*, 193.

[35] Ibid.

[36] Sweet, *Aqua Church*, 80.

recapture the ability to speak the language of the culture, immerse ourselves in the world around us and envision new and creative ways to adapt our communication of the gospel to this new world.

PART II

A Change In Ourselves

Chapter 4

Subculture Blues

I often joke about the fact that I missed the 90s. At the time, I was busy finishing off my seminary education while working in what would be considered a traditional church setting. For me, life consisted almost exclusively of studying and being involved with my church community where I served as one of the associate pastors. The combination of these two responsibilities kept me very busy. And if having a life that was far too busy wasn't bad enough, this was compounded by the fact that I also existed within a very small bubble where I listened almost exclusively to Christian music, was reading books related to my studies and vocation and usually only hung out with other Christians.

This may sound odd to some, but my experience was not that different from that of my fellow students. In fact, not only is this type of experience normative for most individuals who are engaged in vocational ministry, it is the norm for most Christians. Generally speaking, western Christians are immersed in the church subculture. Sometimes this is intentional, other times it is just the result of the subtle trappings that come with being so heavily involved with the church. Regardless of the reasons, the truth is that this is a persistent problem for the church. I know what you are thinking, "this couldn't happen to me, or to my church," but it does. It is a pervasive problem and is one of the biggest reasons why the church is viewed as being so out of touch by the larger society around it. Part of this is because we approach the world with an, 'us and them' mentality. Individuals are either in or out and there is little in between. We think that the aversion of outsiders to church is because they are running from God, but that is only a small part of the picture. The truth is that a lot of the time they are running from us, not God. They just think that we are weird.

The tragedy of this situation is that it is a very normative attitude, both by the church and by those looking at the church from the outside. Dave Kinnaman, in the research and polling of church outsiders which is the foundation of his book *Unchristian*, found that the top five descriptors of Christians by a sample group of non-church goers, with an age range from sixteen to twenty-nine were: judgmental, hypocritical, self-righteous, homophobic and out of touch.[1] These attitudes are becoming more and more normative for those outside of the church and represent a "push back" to the church subculture.

Generally speaking, the church is usually either unaware of these reactions or dismisses opinions like this as being irrelevant and part of a fringe faction. Unfortunately, when this happens what gets lost here is the opportunity to correct these attitudes or even talk about them. Part of the problem that leads to this kind of response is that the church does not realize that it has become a subculture within the larger

---

[1] Kinnaman and Lyons, *Unchristian*, 28.

western cultural milieu. If the church is going to see a successful turn around, it must return to being a counter cultural movement rather than a subculture.

Subculture versus Counterculture

There is a vast difference between the counter culture that we read about in the Bible and subculture that we see expressed in today's faith communities. As a result, in many instances we have forgotten how to relate to those around us who are not part of the church subculture. The old saying that, "you are so heavenly minded you are of no earthly good"[2] applies here. Some Christians spend so much time thinking about what comes after this life that they ignore the fact that life in the here and now is pretty important too!

Without realizing, many Christians have disengaged from being actively involved in the larger cultural context around them. This is a crucial point, because then it affects the way that we go about cultural engagement, if we go about it at all. We often think that we are inviting people to join the countercultural movement of what Jesus is doing but the fact is, we are usually without realizing, asking people to conform to our own church subculture. Many times this happens without us even knowing it.

This happens as the culmination of a series of decisions that seemingly have nothing in common but take us on a path

---

[2] A popular expression used to describe those in the Christian subculture who spend more time thinking about heaven than they do their earthly existence.

60

to almost exclusively identifying with the Christian subculture. The difference between subculture and counterculture can be subtle and we usually don't even realize that it is being expressed. For example, a counter culture says, "be like Jesus," subculture says, "Jesus is like us." Counter culture is concerned with inner motives; subculture is concerned with outward behaviors. Counter culture extols variety, subculture demands conformity. Counter culture engages humanity and challenges the dominant societal cultural expression; subculture barricades itself off from it.

Too often what we don't realize, when we think about attempting to engage the culture around us, is that we are calling people to join the latter instead of the former. Please don't mishear me. I am **not** saying that in order to be effective in the 21st century that the church must be more like the current surrounding culture. On the contrary, I am saying that the church must be less like it and more like the counter cultural movement of pre-Constantinian Christianity.[3] It is a paradox that the church must strive to balance: we have to be like the culture and different from the church all at the same time. Sadly there is no one denomination that seems to have this figured out yet.

Just like every family has its own way of doing things, every church and every denomination has unique qualities that make them different than the others. I have had an

---

[3] Preconstantinian is the term describing the expression of Christianity that was present in the Roman Empire before the emperor Constantine made it a state religion in 313.

uncommonly eclectic journey and have been a part of many different denominations and have first hand experience here. I grew up in the Christian and Missionary Alliance Church. I attended a Lutheran college that had its roots in the Missouri Synod. I had my first pastoral experience in a church affiliated with the Pentecostal Assemblies of Canada. I attended two different Southern Baptist Seminaries for various degrees, spent years ministering and attending churches in the Anglican world and I am now teaching and pastoring with the Canadian National Baptist Convention.

All that to say, there is a vast difference between those tribes. They are all very serious about their faith but they all go about expressing it in very different ways. What might be common or acceptable in one might be frowned upon in another. They all have their own subcultural expressions of the Christian faith. That said, there are churches within all of these denominations that have been able to step outside of their subculture to engage the greater cultural expressions around them.   These churches have discovered the secret of the paradox which faces us and "rather than fighting off culture to protect an insular Christian community, they are fighting for the world to redeem it."[4]

A great example of the counter culture that was demonstrated by the early Christians is attested to in an ancient Roman letter known as the Letter to Diognetus. The letter says:

---

[4] *Unchristian*, 176.

For Christians are not distinguished from the rest of humanity by country, language, or custom. For nowhere do they live in cities of their own, nor do they speak some unusual dialect... But while they live in both Greek and barbarian cities... and follow the local customs in dress and food and other aspects of life, at the same time they demonstrate the remarkable and admittedly unusual character of their own citizenship.

They live in their own countries, but only as aliens; they participate in everything as citizens, and endure everything as foreigners. Every foreign country is their fatherland and every fatherland is foreign. They marry like everyone else, and have children, but they do not destroy their offspring. They share their food but not their wives.

They live on earth, but their citizenship is in heaven. They obey the established laws indeed in their private lives they transcend the laws. They love everyone, and by everyone they are persecuted... They are poor yet they make many rich; they are in need of everything, yet they abound in everything. They are dishonored yet they are glorified in their dishonor; they are slandered yet they are vindicated.[5]

However, within the context of western Christianity this example is not very often the case. All too often, we act like a subset of the dominant culture rather than the counterculture we are meant to be. Gandhi once commented on the difference between these two realities when he said, "I like your Christ, I do not like your Christians, your Christians are so unlike your Christ." Or to put it into more modern terms, "I

---

5 Lightfoot and Harmer, *The Apostolic Fathers*, 299.

like the band; I just can't stand its fans."[6] What Gandhi said back then is still unfortunately and ever increasingly true today. The evidence of this is all around but we are often times not aware of our behavior. Like the addict in need of an intervention we need to have our behaviors pointed out to us.

Ultimately, we are the sum of our decisions. Each day we make decisions that grow into behaviors which gradually shape the path that we are on. Some of these decisions are made for us, like where we went to school as children. Some decisions are deliberate ones that we make for ourselves like spousal choice, where we live or work. In the end, all of these choices have a cumulative effect and dictate what our lives look like. Usually this happens without us even realizing. We don't often analyze life this way, as the culmination of many decisions that have shaped our reality, its just life, we don't know any different. Socrates said that, "an unexamined life is not worth living."[7] The *Flanders Factor Inventory* helps us to examine our lives, our decisions and shows us how and why we have ended up in the place that we now are.

The Flanders Factor Inventory

The *Flanders Factor Inventory* is a rudimentary indicator of Christian enculturation that takes its name from the popular *Simpsons* character. It is a brief lifestyle inventory that I

---

[6] I first heard this quote used by the great Canadian sportscaster and friend Paul Romanuk.

[7] Plato, *The Last Days of Socrates*, 57.

designed in order to illuminate the degree that individuals are submerged in the Christian subculture. The premise is, the higher an individual's score, the more like *Ned Flanders*[8] that person is, and the higher the resonance that individual has with the church subculture.

The inventory illuminates the fact that not only are Christians now part of a distinct subculture, but it also demonstrates the depth to which an individual is immersed in that subculture. What is also highlighted by the inventory is the fact that there is a dichotomy between the prevailing "church culture," and the culture experienced by those in the non-churched component of society. The inventory accomplishes these objectives by asking a series of lifestyle questions that highlight some of the more important life decisions that individuals make or have had made for them and then assigns a measurable value to the answers of those questions. The outcome is one of three results -- a low, medium or high level of Christian enculturation.

If the individual has a score of thirty or less, that represents a relatively low level of Christian enculturation. A low level of Christian enculturation means that individuals in this scoring range have a healthy level of contact with the greater secular culture and have a relatively easy time existing in both this world and the church subculture. Thirty-one to sixty represents a moderate value. Individuals in this range are

---

[8] Ned Flanders is a recurring fictional character in the animated television series *The Simpsons*, created by Matt Groening, and developed by James L. Brooks, Matt Groening and Sam Simon.

immersed in the church subculture to a significant degree and will have to take intentional steps in order to engage the greater secular culture. Sixty-one to one hundred represents a high level of resonance with the church subculture. In this case, individuals are almost completely immersed in the church subculture and have very little meaningful contact with anyone from outside their clique. Individuals with this score will have to make drastic changes to their outlook in order to be able to have any chance of engaging the greater western cultural ethos.

The inventory arrives at these scores by assigning a value to the answers of simple lifestyle questions. These questions come from three basic categories. The first category is made up of choices that were made *for* the individual. That would include things like that person's name, where they went to school, and where or if they went to church as children. The second level of questioning is made up of the choices that we make for ourselves. Examples of questions in this category would include where that person went to college, their occupation, what city they live in or where they go to church. The final level of questions revolves around the choices that the individual has made for others. Examples in this category would include the name of their children or where those children go to church or school. The extrapolation from this data provides us with the individual's score.

What comes from this data is a rudimentary indication of how deeply that individual is immersed in the church subculture. The results have often surprised those who have taken the inventory. We are not usually aware of the cumulative effect that our choices have. It sneaks up on us without our realizing. The old anecdote of how to boil a frog would apply here. If you try to put a frog in a beaker full of boiling water it will instinctively jump out. However, if you put a frog into cold water that is slowly heated, the frog will not immediately react to the change. This is an extreme but effective metaphor because the same could be said for many of us. If we were aware of where some of our life choices would take us, we might make different choices. It's only after we realize where we are and how we got there, that we can make changes to rectify the situation.

Chapter 5

The Church Relevancy Index

The same truths that are discovered on an individual basis in the *Flanders Factor* can be discovered on a corporate level for churches. *The Church Relevancy Index* – a cultural relevancy index that I created – gets its inspiration from a well-known organization which maintains a paid, hour long weekday morning television presence in Canada through the donations of supporters. Starting about seven years ago, while I was working as a personal trainer in Vancouver, I noticed an interesting phenomenon.

Like most gyms, we had our cardio equipment facing a bank of TV monitors so our clients could pass their time by watching television. During the morning appointments, the channels on the various monitors were usually set to either sports or morning news. However, after the morning news on one of the stations was a paid Christian program. I noticed without fail, that whenever this particular program came on my clients would leap for the remotes in order to change the channel as quickly as possible. The painful truth of most Christian broadcasting, is that only the few people who are part of that particular subculture can stand to watch it. And while it is a valuable resource for those who are part of that small subculture, people on the outside of that subculture would rather risk life and limb by scrambling for the TV remote while running on a treadmill.

The index, which is graded out of 100, works on a simple principle. The closer your church's score is to 100, the more like this television program and the church subculture it is -- and the less likely in my opinion, that anybody off the street would be interested in sitting through a Sunday service at your church. The lower the score, the better your church is at engaging the greater Canadian (or American or other) culture and the more likely it is that a first time visitor might return. The index looks at how the church in question is doing in seven basic categories: friendliness, time use, music/visuals, language use, level of Christian enculturation, level of community connection and web presence. The sum of these scores is used to give a rudimentary indication of how likely someone from the community is to visit the church more than once. The lower the score, the more likely that is to happen. The higher the score, the more likely it is that you will never see that person in your church again.

Grading:
13-30/100 - Exceptional
31-60/100 - Good but would benefit from minor
       adjustments.
61-80/100 - Not good
80-100/100 - Major adjustments needed.

The point scoring system is quite simple. In an effort to eliminate as much subjectivity as possible, the index only measures key areas that can be easily identified and measured. The point score is either out of five or ten. The variable in question is then measured by starting at the low or mid or high range depending on the category in question then adding or subtracting points depending on what is being measured.

Friendliness:

Everyone likes to see a friendly face when they show up to a new place, especially if you have summoned up the nerve to go to church. *The Church Relevancy Index* measures a church's friendliness in three key places. These being at the beginning, the middle and the end of the service, for a value out of five for each of the three occasions, for a total of fifteen.

The measurement for each of the segments starts at four and goes up or down depending on the response from the congregant. For instance, the beginning of the service measurement would take place as the visitor walks through the front doors on their way to the sanctuary. Starting at a four, the number would go up or down by a factor of one if they are greeted by an usher or any other congregant; so if they are greeted, the score goes down by one. If they can walk in and get a seat without being greeted, the score goes up by one. If the greeting congregant introduces themselves by name, the number would go down by one again. If this happens more that once, the number would again go down by one to a low score of one.

This process would be again repeated at the midpoint in the service where attendees usually "greet" each other and then again when exiting the church after the service. The mid-service measurement also starts at four. If greeted, one is subtracted. If not greeted, a point of one is added. Again, if the greeting congregant introduces themselves, another point is subtracted. If this happens more than once, one more point is subtracted, to a low of one. When exiting the church, I again start at four and add one point to a high of five if I get out of the church without anyone saying anything to me. If I'm greeted, I subtract one point for each time that someone says goodbye or thanks for coming, to a low of one.

Time Use:

The second item that the index measures is time use. Specifically, how long are the sermon and the overall service? The reason for this is simple: time is the most valuable commodity that we have and no one likes to feel that their time is being abused. You shouldn't leave church thinking to yourself, "well, there is two hours that I'll never get back again." Nevertheless, that is exactly how some individuals feel when they leave church, whether they are first time visitors or long time attendees. The scoring for time use is as follows:

Service Start: I start at one and give a score of one if the service starts on time. If the service does not start on time, I add one point for each minute it is late starting to a high of ten points.

71

Flow of the service: I start at one and add a point for every obviously awkward interruption to the flow of the service to a high of ten points.

Service Length: The grace period for the length of a service is one hour. In my opinion, after that people begin to get restless. To score this category, I start at one and give a score of one if the service is one hour in length. If service goes longer than an hour, I add one point for every five minutes it goes past, to a maximum of ten points.

Sermon Length: The grace period for the length of a sermon is twenty minutes. Again in my opinion, you can't hold too many people's attention on one topic beyond that. To score this category, I start at one and give a score of one if the sermon is twenty minutes in length. If the sermon goes longer than twenty minutes, I add one point for every five minutes it goes past twenty minutes of a maximum of ten points.

Language:

Nobody likes it when they cannot understand what is being said. The temptation to use jargon is a danger that any subculture faces when a group of individuals from that clique are gathered together. This is not a problem for other subcultures because generally speaking it is only the "insiders" who are gathered at the meetings. However, part of the church's mandate is to be accessible for not-yet-Christians as well as those who are part of the church. This cannot happen if visitors are immediately excluded because of the type of language that is used by the worshipping community. This category measures the amount of jargon that is being used. The question is, are you speaking English in the church service or *Christianese*?

To score this category, I start at one and add one point for every few obvious insider terms used to a maximum of ten. Christian jargon is generally made up of any theological or biblical terminology. These are most likely to be lost on those visiting who are not part of the church subculture. I am not saying that a church can't use these terms, but rather I am saying that churches need to be aware that when they use them, they are likely excluding those who are outside of that subculture from the conversation. If there is a way to get the point across without using theological terms, I say do it.

Visuals:

We live in a visual culture. People now hear with their eyes. For this reason, I believe that it is of paramount importance to integrate visuals into all aspects of the service. To score this category, I start at four and add one if no visuals are used (or if they are still using 1970s technology like transparencies on an overhead projector!) to a high of five. If visuals like Power Point are used, I subtract one if used during music, I subtract another point if used during the sermon, and I subtract a final point if video is employed at any point during the service, to a low of one.

Music:

Music taste and preference is very subjective. Rather than focusing on what kind of music is played in a church, the index focuses on how well that music is played. The question is simply, "is it done well, or does it sound like nails on a chalkboard?" Scoring for this category starts at one and goes up by one point to a maximum of five for each of the following questions that are answered affirmatively. First, were the musicians competent? If not then I add a point. Second, if it's a band, did it play well together? If not, a point is added. Third, could the vocalist sing well? Fourth, if more than one vocalist was involved, did they sing well together? If not, then I add a point to a high of five possible points.

Level of Christian Enculturation:

The index seeks to answer the question of whether most of your church's energy and resources are inward or outward in focus. It's a question of maintenance versus mission. Scoring for this category starts at one and goes up by a point for every activity, outside of those that take place on Sunday, designed for the edification of the church attendees. e.g. Lady's morning out, bible studies, small groups, men's breakfast etc.

Level of Community Connection:

The index seeks to answer two key questions here. First, how involved in the community is your church? And second, is your church missional, (going out to the community), or attractional, (devising ways to get the community to come to you), in its mindset? Scoring for this category starts at ten and one point is deducted for every example of community involvement and an extra point is deducted if that interaction happens outside of the church building, to a low of one.

Web Presence:

The index asks four questions about a church's web presence. First, is it web 2.0 or is it from the 90s? Second, is it easily navigated? Third, does it have all the information that I need? Fourth, does it contain media resources, i.e. streaming audio or video? The thought behind rating a church's web page is that the average person will go to a web page long before they enter your building. Their first impression of your church will be made there, so if your web page is not very good it is very likely that you will not see them at your church. Scoring for this category starts at a five and one point is deducted for every box that is ticked to a low of one.

Churches, like the individuals measured by the *Flanders Factor Inventory,* are often unaware of their behaviors and what may be keeping them from having any appeal to the community around them. They are used to what they do and how they do it and like any family, become accustomed to the idiosyncrasies and quirks that are part of their community expression. *The Church Relevancy Index* provides congregations with an outsider's view of their community and the weaknesses that those in the community might not otherwise notice. On the other hand, it also provides churches with a fresh look at what they are doing particularly well – that they may not even realize.

To help explain the index further, here are two examples of the Church Relevancy Index at work. These are two churches that I have recently put through the index and because they are on opposite sides of the spectrum, they'll provide a good idea of what the index seeks to highlight.

Church A

Church A is an example of a church on the high end of the index. Although it has come in with a mid-grade, in many categories like Friendliness, Visuals, Music and Web Presence it has lost valuable points in the weightier categories.

The first of these was the heavily jargoned language used. From the beginning of the service it heavily employed theological language, and as a result ended up scoring a nine out of ten on the index. The next category that it scored high in was the sermon length, which was sixty-five minutes long. The reality of this category is that there is very few pastors who are gifted enough as public speakers to hold an audience for that length of time. As a result, this church had one point added for every five minutes past the twenty-minute mark, for a score of ten out of ten. A good rule of thumb is, if in doubt, err on the side of caution and try to be as concise as possible.

76

People are more likely to forgive for being too short than too long.

The final two categories that this church had high scores on were Christian Enculturation and Community Connection. They scored high in the category of Christian Enculturation because the programs that they promoted in the bulletin and in the church service seemed to be more maintenance than mission in orientation, so they gained one point for each to a high score of ten out of ten. In the category of Community Connection, this church only had two programs or initiatives that were designed solely for the purpose of being a blessing to the community around them so they scored an eight out of ten. As a result of these shortcomings, this church scored a seventy-nine out of one hundred, and in my opinion, would need a significant adjustment to its church expression to be effective in appealing to the Canadian cultural dynamic.

Church 'A' Score

Friendliness: Greeting/Conversation/Goodbye: 3/3/4 for a total of 10/15.

Service: Start/Flow/Length: 6/8/9 for a total of 23/30.

Language: 9/10.

Sermon Length: 10/10.

Visuals: 3/5.

Music: 3/5.

Level of Christian Enculturation: 10/10.

Level of Community Connection: 8/10.

Web Presence: 3/5.

Total: 79/100

Church B

Church B did not do as well as Church A in the friendliness category, but had better marks in every other category, and is not too far away from being rated in the "exceptional" range. Friendliness seems to be an issue for this church. The fact that no one spoke to me at all before, during or after the service, except the pastor as I was leaving, is a huge issue for this church. Frankly, you cannot expect people to feel welcome at your church if those who attend the church are not welcoming! This is the front line in a church being seen as approachable and is usually the easiest to fix.

However, as a result of its standoffishness, this church's marks for friendliness were quite high. On the other hand, there were many things that this church did well. Although the service was late in starting, it did have a good flow with a minimal number of unnecessary interruptions. The length of the service was also good coming in at an hour and twenty minutes, so netting a score of five out of ten. Another positive for this church is that it spoke English, not *Christianese,* during the service, so the language marks were low. It scored a two out of ten in the language category. The sermon was concise, only 25 minutes, scoring a two out of ten.

The other strong aspects of the service were the facts that the pastor used visual media and integrated it with expertise throughout the service; and it has a great web presence, scoring one out of five in each of the respective categories. Besides the friendliness category, the only place that it could use some work is, like church A, in the categories of Christian Enculturation and Community Connection, which means that it is still more maintenance-minded than missional, and bit more attractional than incarnational, having more programs that service the church membership than the community. As stated earlier, this church is well on its way to a ranking of "exceptional" and with a few minor adjustments would easily move into this category.

Church 'B' Score

Friendliness: Greeting/Conversation/Goodbye: 5/5/1 for a total of 11/15.

Service: Start/Flow/Length: 7/4/5 for a total of 16/30.

Language: 2/10.

Sermon Length: 2/10

Visuals: 1/5.

Music: 1/5.

Level of Christian Enculturation: 7/10.

Level of Community Connection: 7/10.

Web Presence: 1/5.

Total: 48/100

Chapter 6

Making Contact

In the midst of the fog that we now find ourselves in, there are a growing number of churches that have realized there is a problem with the status quo. They're seeking opportunities to authentically connect in contextual and tangible ways with the communities around them. The size of the churches varies but their method is always the same. They all approach the issue of cultural engagement from an incarnational, missional/relational and adaptive perspective. Their expression of faith isn't restricted to "religious" activities, but carries over into every day of the week and each aspect of the church life.[1]

These faith communities actively seek ways that they can be a blessing to their communities. They are endeavoring to be a blessing without agenda or strings. They choose to be a blessing *in spite of* whether or not they see more people from the community showing up on any given Sunday, not because of it. They realize that the beauty of the Gospel is displayed in both word and deed and seek ways that they can demonstrate this principle to the communities around them.

These churches take the charge of St. Francis seriously when he said, "preach the gospel to all the world, and if

---

[1] Lyons, *The Next Christians*, 48.

necessary, use words."[2] They take a pragmatic approach to their work and start by doing what is necessary, then do what is possible, and suddenly they are doing the impossible.[3] Though there are many churches that are doing great things, here are three churches of varying sizes that provide examples from what is happening on the west coast of Canada and the United States. By providing three different sized churches, it should be apparent that churches of any size can see these principles work. These churches are, (in ascending order of size): Ion Community in North Vancouver, Canada; New Hope Church in Calgary, Canada and Imago Dei in Portland, Oregon.

Ion Community

Ion community is a network of small churches located in the greater metropolitan area of Vancouver, British Columbia, Canada. The vision of Ion is to start a multi-nucleated network of churches in the various city and municipal centers across the Lower Mainland. This vision, coupled with Ion's desire to be a blessing to its communities, flows from the vision of the lead pastor Sean Benesh. For Sean, the desire was to create

---

[2] A famous quote most often attributed to St. Francis of Assisi available from http://www.quotesdaddy.com/author/St.+Francis+of+Assisi. Accessed March 1, 2011.

[3] A famous quote most often attributed to St. Francis of Assisi available from http://www.quotesdaddy.com/author/St.+Francis+of+Assisi. Accessed March 1, 2011.

faith communities that were contextual, creative, walkable, communal and simple.

These communities are focused on the transformation of the neighborhoods in which they are located. For the North Vancouver campus, the main initiative that facilitates this vision is called urthTREK. North Vancouver sits in the shadows of the Coastal Mountains and is a very outdoor-orientated community. However, these pursuits are often times beyond the means of the average family. urthTREK is an outdoor adventure non-profit that focuses on individuals of lower income and the marginalized. urthTREK connects people with outdoor adventures and gives them their first experience whether that is through longboarding, hiking, mountain biking, advocacy or environmental education. urthTREK is about giving others memorable exposure to outdoor adventure whether that be through actually hitting the trail to outdoor education, meeting local outdoor athletes or urban advocacy. urthTREK is a multi-pronged approach to introducing youth in North Vancouver to these pursuits by providing a subsidized and cost effective exposure to these activities. Currently there are three main features to Urthtrek that facilitate the vision behind it. These are: Lids for Kids, the Long Boarding Club and the Bicycle Repair Course.

Lids for Kids

Lids for Kids is an initiative to provide bicycle or skateboarding helmets for children who don't have one.

82

According so Sean, "we want to see our children live an active and healthy lifestyle. Helmets are proven to save lives and we believe that children deserve the best that we can offer." This initiative provides a tangible expression of Ion's concern for the community of North Vancouver.

Longboarding Club

Vancouver has a very mild climate and for this reason activities like skate boarding are extremely popular. In fact, many individuals use longboards as a mode of commuting. The after-school long boarding club for elementary students is designed to give children who might not be able to afford it, the basics of longboarding. In this class, students get all the basics of how to ride a longboard. It is open to all and for those who do not have a long board, one is provided for them and they will get to keep the long board that they use during the class.

Bicycle Repair Course

Mountain biking is a way of life in Vancouver. Because of the temperate climate and the wealth of bike trails, both off road and on, people literally use their bikes all year around. However, using a bike this much leads to the inevitable issue of maintenance. The bicycle repair course teaches individuals to do the maintenance themselves so that they can ride a safe bike while avoiding the expensive repair bills that go with it.

Ion's strength is its organic connection to the communities that it inhabits. Though it is a network of small churches it has garnered much influence in these communities because of its authentic love for them. If Ion were to be compared to an animal, it would be an ant. Ants are much stronger than they look, being able to lift many times their own weight. Likewise, Ion wields more influence than many much larger churches, through its authentic community connection.

New Hope Church

New Hope Church is a medium-sized church[4] in Calgary, Alberta, which was planted fifteen years ago by John Van Sloten. The church operates out of the community center located in the inner city neighborhood of West Hillhurst. As part of its make up, New Hope seeks ways to be a blessing to the community around it. The leadership team realizes that in a twenty-first century context, demonstrating the gospel is just as important as proclaiming it.

The leadership realizes that you don't have to do it all alone or create new church programs to see this happen. They believe that you can partner with organizations that are already active and working in the neighborhood. In order to facilitate this value, New Hope intentionally involves itself with many community agencies and programs. Some of these include help and support to local seniors groups, promoting,

---

[4] A medium sized church in Canada is a church that has between 200 and 500 hundred people in weekly attendance.

supporting and being involved with area kids programs and connecting with neighborhood programs like *Inn From the Cold*[5] and *Neighbour Link*.[6] These latter two initiatives are very important because the church is located in an inner city setting and the issue of homelessness is prevalent, as it is in most major North American cities. In all of these activities, New Hope strives to be a blessing and serves as a great example of what it means to love and serve your community. However, New Hope's strongest quality flows from John and the way that he goes about engaging culture, specifically through his sermons.

John is incarnational in his outlook and preaching. In fact, John is a master of what can be referred to as *incarnational preaching*.[7] He is passionate in his belief that God is speaking to us all the time and occasionally this might be through, what some might think are unorthodox sources. He operates under the premise that all truth is God's truth[8] and has an uncanny ability to see God at work all around him in everyday life.

---

[5] *Inn From the Cold* provides "emergency shelter, support and programs to homeless children, their families and others in need, with the goal of building healthy, stable families and ending homelessness." http://www.innfromthecold.org/our-story.

[6] "*Neighbourlink* is a non-profit organization that provides neighbours in need with practical help and basic resources by linking them to a network of community donors and volunteers who care." http://neighbourlinkcalgary.com.

[7] Incarnation Preaching is preaching out of the observations of God and encounters with God that we see all around us.

[8] Van Sloten, *The Day Metallica Came To Church*, 149.

Whether it is the concept of justice contained in a *Metallica* song,[9] the truth about the human condition as found in the movie *Crash,* [10] or the basic need for connection as evidenced by the explosion of social networking sites like *Facebook,*[11] John notices how God is working through culture and then draws insightful correlations between those observed divine truths and how God revealed these truths in the Bible.

John maintains that we see what we are looking for,[12] and John sees God at work all around him. He looks for and finds God involved in everyday life and then communicates those observed truths from the pulpit. As a result of his theocentric outlook toward culture and his innovative preaching style, John has received much attention from the media. He has been interviewed by various television, radio and newspaper outlets over the years and finally turned the whole experience into a book, *The Day Metallica Came To Church*, in 2010.

Through this exposure, New Hope has been able to engage and connect with those who might not go to, or have ever been to a church, in a way that few churches do. New Hope is a brilliant example of how a medium sized church can effectively engage culture in the twenty-first century. By using

---

[9] Ibid., 16.

[10] Ibid., 106.

[11] From the sermon, "Finding God Through Facebook," by John Van Sloten. March 6, 2010.

[12] *The Day Metallica Came To Church*, 154.

its own resources, coupled with those in the community and John's ability to observe biblical truths in everyday life, it has had a profound impact on the community and city.

Imago Dei Church

Imago Dei is a large church in Portland, Oregon planted over ten years ago by Rick McKinley. Like both the Ion Community in Vancouver and New Hope in Calgary, Imago excels at loving and serving the community surrounding it. However, because Imago is a very large church it doesn't focus on a specific neighborhood in Portland. It looks at the quadrants of Southeast and Northeast Portland as being its main community.

Of the many programs that Imago has created in order to facilitate this value, a few programs stand out as being particularly altruistic and missional in their focus. These are: the *Love Portland* program, the *Local Outreach* focus, the *Missional Grants* initiative and *Vibe Portland*. All of these programs have been put in place to focus on giving back to the community for the sake of the community regardless of whether or not it creates converts. They are practicing the concept of being blessed in order to be a blessing. This concept of reciprocal blessing is something that is near and dear to the vision of Imago. In fact, Rick McKinley models this concept well in the way he pastors Imago Dei. Instead of measuring its success based on Sunday-morning attendance, the church quantifies its success by how many of its congregants are involved in restoring the city of Portland.[13]

Love Portland

Love Portland is an initiative that focuses on the schools of Portland. Specifically, it is a program that provides nutritious lunches at no cost for the students in the low-income neighborhoods and schools that surround Imago. This program has had a profound impact on the community. It has even garnered attention from municipal politicians who have praised the program and the church's involvement with the area schools.[14] When the larger community realizes that the church wants to be a blessing and help that community to be better, the community always responds in a positive way.

Local Outreach

This aspect of Imago's make up is particularly interesting. Instead of classifying "outreach" as something that is done by church members in order to entice those they have contact with back to the church, which is ultimately an inward concentration, Imago's focus is strictly outward, with an expectation on every church member to be involved in his or her community in some way. Imago says that, "by striving to meet specific neighbors in Portland with Christ's love tailored

---

[13] *The Next Christians*, 159-160.

[14] LePort, "Imago Dei's 'Love Portland' Program."

to them, God's mission becomes Imago's action. And by sharing about how Christ is leading His people personally and collectively, despite specific weaknesses and sins, God's journey becomes recognizable as a human journey."[15] It is this intentionality coupled with Imago's desire to be a blessing to those around it that has helped it to enjoy such a favorable standing with both its direct community of influence and the city of Portland.

Missional Grants

The *Missional Grant* program began with a simple premise, "what if we spent less and gave more during Christmas in order to worship fully?"[16] Specifically, the leadership at Imago asked the question, "how do we love the unloved and serve the marginalized?" The *Missional Grant* program provides funds for individuals with an idea on how to be a blessing to those in the community. It doesn't matter if the idea is for-profit, non-profit, church or neighborhood based. Imago has grants available to individuals who want to make a difference in their neighborhood.

---

[15] Information on Imago's Local Outreach initiative is available from http://www.imagodeicommunity.com/article/missional-community-overview

[16] Information on Imago's Missional Grant initiative is available from http://www.imagodeicommunity.com/article/missional-grants.

Vibe of Portland

One of the first things to be cut from any educational budget in the public schools when money is tight is the arts program. *Vibe of Portland* is an initiative designed to support and develop the arts in neighborhoods without such programs. Imago believes that art and music can inspire and beautify us all. It believes that "the arts instill a sense of worth, belonging and discipline in those who participate."[17] Unfortunately, this opportunity is missing for many students in the Portland area because music and art have been reduced or eliminated in many of the schools, especially those in lower income neighborhoods. With this program, Imago fills an important gap in the educational experience of Portland students that would otherwise be neglected.

Imago is a great example of a large church that has a passion for the community around it and desires to communicate the Gospel in both word and deed. Through its various community initiatives, Imago has had a profound impact on Portland and has demonstrated God's love for that city time and time again.

Though they are different sizes and in different cities, what these three churches have in common is a desire to be a blessing in and to their communities. Though the specifics of what they do vary, they all go about their calling in an incarnational, missional/relational and adaptive way. They all

---

[17] Information on Vibe of Portland is available from http://www.imagodeicommunity.com/article/vibe-of-portland.

seek ways that they can have a holistic[18] impact in their communities. They all strive to fix the broken and restore their realm of immediate influence to that which God has intended. It is a difficult but rewarding process, which has been embraced by churchgoers and non-churchgoers alike. In an age where secular society is just not that into the church, these churches have found ways to connect with their neighborhoods and cities in tangible and vital ways. As a result, people are very much into these churches, and the Christian expression that they bring with them.

---

[18] Holistic restoration seeks to fix the whole problem, relational, socio-economic, and emotional rather than just focusing on the spiritual aspect of life as has been the focus of Christianity for the last 150 years.

Chapter 7

A World Without Limits

There is a well-known self-help mantra that says, "the first step toward recovery is admitting that you have a problem." The church has a problem. The first part of this problem is that the world has changed and it has not.

In our current situation, we are seeing a societal shift from the modern to postmodern age and whether we realize it or not, it is affecting every aspect of life in western civilization. What is alarming is that to this point the church in the western world has largely ignored these monumental changes. For this reason, the western church has experienced a dramatic decrease in both its effectiveness and influence in the last fifty years. The tried and true methodologies that once worked are becoming less and less effective with each passing year.

In addition, during this time of transition, the church in the western world has retreated into itself and become a subculture of the greater culture around it. We have sentenced ourselves to live in a Christian ghetto, cut off from the larger cultural expression. Ultimately though, the blame for this situation falls on the church leadership. It seems to be addicted to doing church the same way that it has in decades past and perpetuating a model of cultural engagement that is no longer able to effectively influence the larger culture around it. The truth, whether we want to hear it or not, is that those who are part of the secular western cultural expression are simply not that into us, and the sooner we acknowledge this, the sooner we will be able to move into the future and begin to address the complex issues that face western culture today.

The primary purpose of this book was to address this problem and take a small, tangible step toward embracing a model of engagement that will once again effectively communicate the gospel to Canadians and others within 'western' milieu. The hope is that by taking steps to recognize where the church is in relation to the greater western culture, the church will be better able to position itself to once again be a vital and positive influence. It is my belief that if we adopt a model of cultural engagement that is incarnational, missional/ relational and adaptive that we will be better able to navigate these cultural obstacles we find before us. After all, the biggest obstacle facing the church today should be one that is easily removed: its own resistance to change.

Let us be bold enough and brave enough to admit that we have a problem and embrace and engage this new world that we now find ourselves in. If we are going to be all that God wants us to be, then we must not shrink back in fear of this change. Likewise, we cannot expect those in the world to come to us. We must find ways to go and connect with them, and take God's message of life and love to a hurting and dying world.

Appendix 1

The Flanders Factor Inventory

Full Name:

Occupation:

Current city of residence:

Number of countries that you have lived in:

Relationally Involved: yes/no:
If yes where did you meet your spouse/partner/boy/girlfriend?

Is your spouse/partner/boy/girlfriend the same ethnic
background as you are?

Kids: yes/no:
If yes what school do they go to?

Current Church:

Number of years attending that church:

Current Church's Affiliation:

Number of years that you have been affiliated with that
denomination:

List the last three Churches that you have attended and their
affiliation:

Number of times per week you are in a "church" building:

Name of the church that my parents go to:

First names of three of your closest friends and the churches that they go to:

Name of your High School:

Name of your Post-Secondary Institution(s):

Favorite song right now:

Favorite band right now:

Favorite book:

What are you reading right now:

First names of your neighbors on either side of your home:

Appendix 2

The Flanders Factor Inventory Key

Full Name: *5 points for 2 biblical names, 3 points for 1, and 1 point for none.*

Occupation: *5 points for full time ministry, 3 points for bi-vocational work, and 1 point for secular work.*

Current city of residence: *5 points if that's your home town, 3 points if it's in a different province/state than you grew up in, and 1 point if it's in a different country than you grew up in.*

Number of countries that you have lived in: *5 points for 1, 3 points for 2, and 1 point for three or more.*

Relationally Involved: yes/no:
If yes where did you meet your spouse/partner/boy/girlfriend? *5 points if you met your partner at your church, 3 points if at a different church than yours or church orientated activity, and 1 point for anywhere else.*

Is your spouse/partner/boy/girlfriend the same ethnic background as you are? *5 points for same ethnicity same country of origin, 3 points for different ethnicity but born in the same country, and 1 point for different ethnicity and different country of origin.*

Kids: yes/no:
If yes what school do they go to? *5 points if they go to a Christian school, 3 points if it has "St." in the name, and 1 point for public school.*

Current Church:
Number of years attending that church: *5 points if you have been in that church for more than 5 years, 3 points if you have been in that church for between 2 and 5 years, and 1 point if you have been in that church for less than a year.*

Current Church's Affiliation:
Number of years that you have been affiliated with your current denomination: *5 points if you have been in that denomination for more than 5 years, 3 points if you have been in that denomination for between 2 and 5 years, and 1 point if you have been in that denomination for less than a year.*

List the last three Churches that you have attended and their affiliation: *5 points if all 3 are in the same denomination, 3 points if 2 are in the same denomination, and 1 point if all three are in different denominations.*

Number of times per week you are in a "church" building: *5 points for 3 or more, 3 points for twice a week, and 1 point for one time per week or less.*

Name of the church that my parents go to: *5 points if that is your current church, 3 points if you go to a different church in the same denomination, and 1 point for different church in a different denomination.*

First names of three of your closest friends and the churches that they go to: *5 points all three currently go to the same church as you, 3 points if all three go to church, and 1 point of one or more them are not Christians.*

Name of your High School: *5 points if it was a Christian school, 3 points if it had "St." in the name, and 1 point for public school.*

Name of your Post Secondary Institution(s): *5 points if one or more are Christian school, 3 points if you have been to multiple institutions and one has been a Christian school, and 1 point if you went to a secular post secondary institution.*

Favorite song right now: *5 points if it a Christian song, and 1 point if is a song by a secular artist.*
Favorite band right now: *5 points if it a Christian band, and 1 point if is a secular band.*

Favorite book: *5 points you said "the bible", or one of the books of the bible, 3 points if was written by a Christian author, and 1 point if it is a secular book.*
What are you reading right now: *5 points you said "the bible", or one of the books of the bible, 3 points if was written by a Christian author, and 1 point if it is a secular book.*

First names of your neighbors on either side of your home. *5 points if you don't know either, 3 points if you know one, and 1 point if you know both.*

100 points possible.
Below 30 points indicates mild Christian enculturation.[19]
From 31 – 60 points indicates moderate level Christian enculturation.
More than 61 points indicates a high level of Christian enculturation.

---

[19] For the grading of the *Flanders Factor* inventory I used a simplified bell curve with three distinct sections: below average, average / moderate, and above average / high.

Appendix 3

The Church Relevancy Index

The Church Relevancy Index is scored out of one hundred and bases its marks on the answers to some simple questions on a variety of subjects.

Friendliness: 15 possible points

Greeting:	/5
Conversations:	/5
Goodbyes:	/5

Use of My Time (was it used and abused?): 40 possible points

Service:	
Start:	/10
Flow:	/10
Length:	/10
Sermon Length:	/10

Visuals and Music: 10 possible points

Music:	/5
Visuals:	/5

Language and Level of Christian Enculturation: 20 possible points

Jargon	/10
Maintenance vs Mission	/10

Level of Community Connection: 10 possible points

Attractional vs Missional	/10

Web Presence: 5 possible points

Web 2.0 vs Web 1.0	/5

Bibliography

Berger, Peter L. and Thomas Luckmann, *The Social Construction of Reality: A Treatise in the Sociology of Knowledge* (London: Penguin, 1991).

Bergquist, Linda and Allan Karr, *Church Turned Inside Out: A Guide for Designers, Refiners, and Re-Aligners* (San Francisco: Jossey-Bass, 2010).

Blackaby, Henry T. and Claude V. King, *Experiencing God: Knowing and Doing the Will of God* (Nashville: Broadman & Holman Publishers, 1994).

Blomberg, Craig, L., *Matthew, The New American Commentary,* ed. David S. Dockery (Nashville: Broadman, 1992).

_____, *1 Corinthians, The NIV Application Commentary,* edited by Terry Muck. (Grand Rapids: Zondervan, 1995).

Bricker, Darrell J., *What Canadians Think* (Toronto: Doubleday, 2005).

Burge, Gary M., *John, NIV Application Commentary*, ed. Terry Muck (Grand Rapids, Michigan: Zondervan, 2000).

Carson, D.A., *The Gospel According to John* (Grand Rapids: Eerdmans, 1991).

Dylan, Bob, *The Times They Are A-Changin'* (New York: Columbia Records, 1964).

Fee, Gordon D., *The First Epistle to the Corinthians, The New International Commentary on the New Testament* (Grand Rapids: Eerdmans, 1987).

Frost, Michael and Alan Hirsch, *The Shaping of Things to Come: Innovation and Mission for the 21st-Century Church* (Peabody: Hendrickson, 2003).

Garland, David E., *1 Corinthians, Baker Exegetical Commentary on the New Testament*, ed. Robert W. Yarbrough and Robert H. Stein (Grand Rapids: Eerdmans, 2003).

Green, Michael, *Evangelism in the Early Church* (Grand Rapids: Eerdmans, 2004).

Grenz, Stanley J., *A Primer on Postmodernism* (Grand Rapids: Eerdmans, 1996).

Hagner, Donald A. *Matthew 14-28, Word Biblical Commentary*, ed. by David A. Hubbard and Glen W. Barker (Dallas: Word Books, 1995).

Halter, Hugh and Matt Smay, *The Tangible Kingdom: Creating Incarnational Community* (San Francisco: Jossey-Bass, 2008).

Hirsch, Alan, *The Forgotten Ways: Reactivating the Missional Church* (Grand Rapids: Brazos Press, 2006).

Hunter, George G. III, *The Celtic Way of Evangelism: How Christianity Can Reach the West ... Again* (Nashville: Abingdon, 2000).

Jézégou, Frédérick, "Quotations by Albert Einstein", http://www.dictionary-quotes.com/in-the-middle-of-difficulty-lies-opportunity-albert-einstein (accessed January 6, 2010).

Kinnaman, David and Gabe Lyons, *Unchristian: What a New Generation Really Thinks about Christianity ... and Why It Matters* (Grand Rapids: Baker, 2007).

Leger Marketing, "How Canadians Perceive Various Professions" (Toronto: Canadian Press, 2003).

LePort, Brian, "Imago Dei's 'Love Portland' Program," *Portland Evangelical Examiner*, 17 August 2009. From examiner.com accessed March 2, 2011.

Lightfoot, J. B. and J. R. Harmer, translators, *The Apostolic Fathers*, ed. Michael W. Holmes (Grand Rapids: Baker Books, 1989).

Lyons, Gabe, *The Next Christians: Seven Ways You Can Live the Gospel and Restore the World* (New York: Doubleday, 2010).

McNeal, Reggie, *Missional Renaissance: Changing the Scorecard for the Church* (San Francisco: Jossey-Bass, 2009).

Plato, *The Last Days of Socrates*, trans. Christopher Rowe (New York: Penguin, 2010).

Raschke, Carl, *GloboChrist: The Great Commission Takes a Postmodern Turn* (Grand Rapids: Baker Academic, 2008).

Reid, Alvin, *Introduction to Evangelism* (Nashville: Broadman & Holman, 1998).

Richardson, Rick, *Evangelism Outside the Box: New Ways to Help People Experience the Good News* (Downers Grove: InterVarsity, 2000).

Sine, Tom, *The New Conspirators: Creating the Future One Mustard Seed at a Time* (Downers Grove: InterVarsity, 2008).

Sire, James W., *Naming the Elephant: Worldview as a Concept* (Downers Grove: InterVarsity, 2004).

Statistics Canada 2006. "Population Distribution of Vancouver, B.C." Census of Canada, http://www12.statcan.gc.ca (accessed 21 October 2009).

Sweet, Leonard, *Soul Tsunami* (Grand Rapids: Zondervan, 1999).

_____, *Aqua Church: Essential Leadership Arts for Piloting Your Church in Today's Fluid Culture* (Loveland: Group, 1999).

_____, *So Beautiful: Divine Design for Life and Church* (Colorado Springs: David C. Cook Publishers, 2009).

Turner, David L., *Matthew, Baker Exegetical Commentary on the New Testament,* ed. Robert W. Yarbrough and Robert H. Stein (Grand Rapids: Eerdmans, 2008).

Van Sloten, John*, The Day Metallica Came To Church: Searching for the Everywhere God in Everything*, Kindle edition (Grand Rapids: Square Inch, 2010).

Webber, Robert E., *The Younger Evangelicals: Facing the Challenges of the New World* (Grand Rapids: Baker, 2002).

Wilkins, Michael J., *Matthew, NIV Application Commentary*, ed. Terry Muck (Grand Rapids: Zondervan, 2004).

About the Author

Stephen Harper is a futurist, a postmodern pilgrim and an educator. He holds a Doctorate from Golden Gate Baptist Theological Seminary, which focuses on envisioning creative ways to connect people with God in the 21st century. In the past, he has worked as a pastor in a variety of settings, and spent 7 years working as a personal trainer and an urban missionary in Vancouver, British Columbia. He has recently relocated to Calgary, Alberta, accepting a teaching position at Rocky Mountain College. He also worked as lead researcher on the Global Television documentary *Hip 2B Holy*, which looked at the re-imagining of Evangelicalism in Canada.

About Urban Loft Publishers

Urban Loft Publishers focuses on ideas, topics, themes, and conversations about all-things *urban*. Urban, or the city, is the central theme and focus for what we publish. In light of rapid urbanization and dense globalization comes the need to continue to hammer out a theology of the city, as well as the impetus to adapt and model urban ministry to the changing twenty-first century city. It is our intention to continue to mix together urban ministry, theology, urban planning, architecture, transportation planning, and the social science as we push the conversation forward about *renewing the city*. While we lean heavily in favor towards scholarly and academic works, we also explore the fun and light side of cities as well. Welcome to the *new* urban world.

www.theurbanloft.org

14143418R00055

Made in the USA
Charleston, SC
23 August 2012